Dumber Verses And Curses

Dumber Verses And Curses

By
Mark H. Glissmeyer

Gradina Books

This book imitates a work of historical fiction. Any resemblance to actual persons, living or dead, should just be forgotten.

Copyright © 2019 by Mark H. Glissmeyer

All rights reserved.

No part of this book may be reproduced, or stored in a retrieval system, or transmitted in any form or by any means, electronic, mechanical, recording, photocopying, or otherwise, without the express written consent of the publisher.

ISBN-13: 978-0-9985416-6-2

Dedication:

This dedication is to words that rhyme
Which try telling the story of our time.

Warning:

Be cautious and strap yourself in
Because like indigestion
Now we begin.

It seems everyone gets a tattoo
From the skinny to the fat ones too
They're placed on their toes
And up by their nose
Or even where they sit down too.

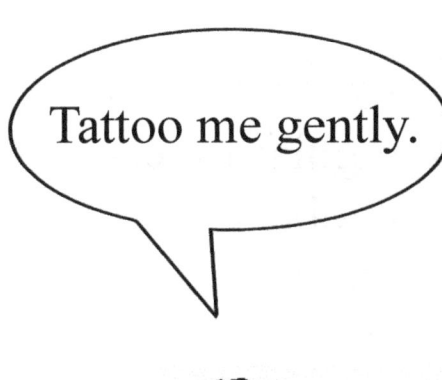
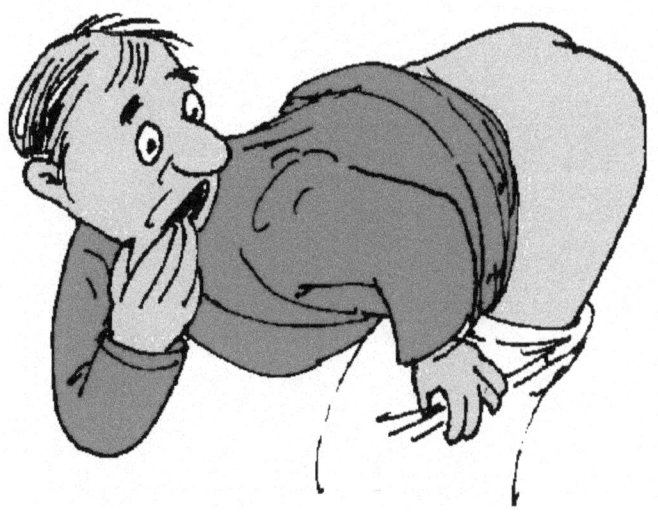

Vaping is the new way for smokers
To impress like the regular tokers
But it seems like tobacco
Which will need a big back hoe
To cover up all of the croakers.

Statement:

The criminals who once got away
Are now sad that we have DNA.

HEADLINE NEWS

Another cold case was cracked thanks to DNA and genetics...

In boxing they now have both genders
And some of them end up contenders
But if it's a knockout
After a sockout
They're regarded as only pretenders.

Statement:

I never thought this book would sell
So if you're reading it, I'm shocked as hell.

We just had another school shooting
While congress all sat around hooting
Without passing a law
They only would jaw
So they certainly deserve a good booting.

Voters:

Before ballots go in the deposit
Beware of skeletons in their closet.

After everyone bought eToys for Christmas
They ended up right out of business
It made children sad
And Santa got mad
Since nothing was left for his mistress.

We are still waiting for delivery from Santa....

Statement:

If sometimes my words never rhyme
It's because I ran out of time.

They're saying with all of this heat
Our sea level will rise twenty feet
I don't know why
Cause outside it's dry
And so far I'm still walking the street.

Drones are more popular it's said
Yet they still aren't very widespread
But they tell us someday
Our mail comes this way
I hope it doesn't drop on my head.

Watch out! Another drone delivery.

Question:

If it was the war to end all wars
Then why do we have any more?

When emailing first began
There wasn't too much spam
But as time went by
And we all know why
It changed into a way to scam.

When emailing first began
There wasn't too much spam
But as time went by
And we all know why
It changed into a way to scam.

Statement:

It's like every two years we see these
When election signs sprout up like trees.

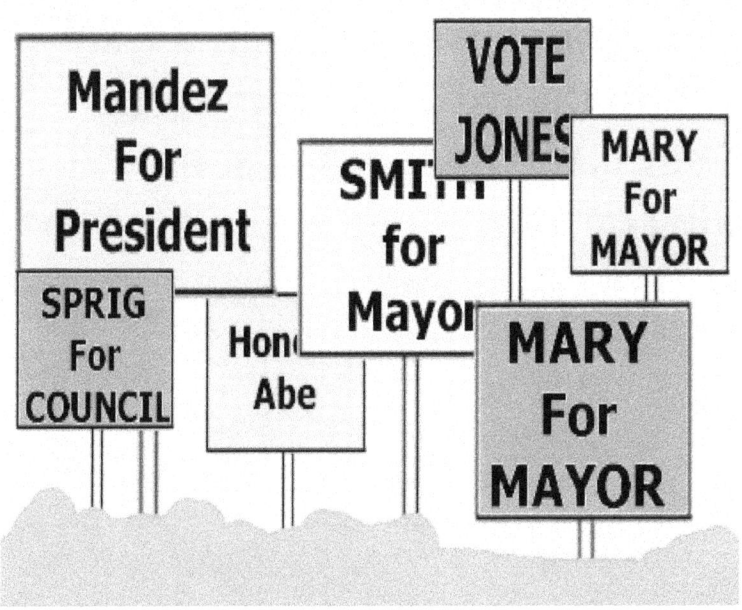

We once were scared of Peak Oil
But found way more in the soil
So the experts were wrong
And cried a sad song
While consumers enjoyed all the spoils.

HEADLINE NEWS

Gasoline prices keep falling due to a glut in oil production...

When we see a doctor for our ills
They'll prescribe us many pills
But some are a dud
When they go in our blood
While the bad ones give us our thrills.

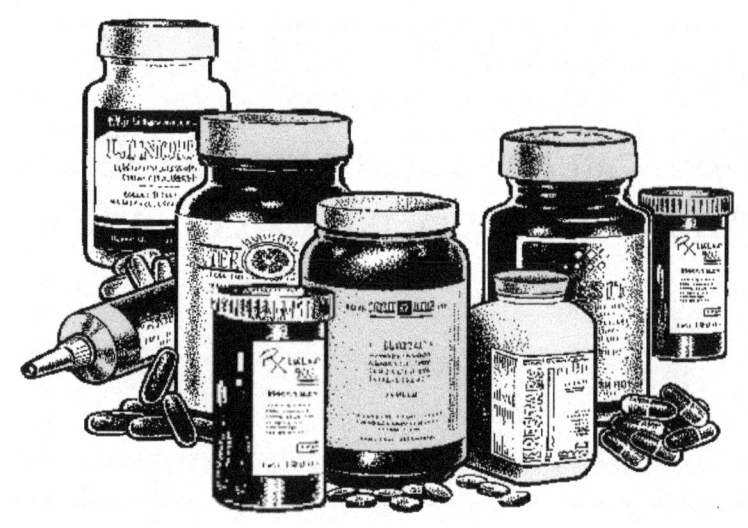

Opioid Epidemic

Flight MA370:

How can a modern plane disappear
And leave every passenger in fear?

Caution:

Don't let pets go in the wild
Or they may eat you in a while.

Florida Everglades

Judiciary:

Why does our only Supreme Court
Give rulings that make us grow warts?

Phone scammers:

The FCC still hasn't blocked any calls
That has users climbing up walls.

Hello, I am calling because your internet will be suspended unless you pay us right away! Press one to pay now!

Caution:

They may have named it fast food
But slowly it has to be chewed.

Ever since I was a young lad
The weather forecasting's been bad
Whether it's sunny or rainy
They're so off it's zany
I just wish it didn't make everyone mad.

Musicians:

Someday your career just might crater
If your music gets played in an elevator.

NASA once went to the moon
But today they seem full of gloom
There are no more rockets
Or dough in their pockets
Let's hope they do something soon.

They talk about women's soccer
With a player who's also a talker
So after winning today
She wants equal pay
While online are those that mock her.

HEADLINE NEWS

U.S. women win World Cup for Fourth title

A virus that's called Wanna Cry
Was created by one crazy guy
He wasn't too handsome
And asked for a ransom
I'm glad I never found out why.

Shopping:

We all have a finite amount of money
If you don't believe me, go ask your honey.

They tell us that self driving cars
Will be good for people in bars
Since once they are tipsy
They won't be a gypsy
And walk home under the stars.

What are they doing with genes
Which they edit, whatever that means
They promised we'll grow stronger
And our lives will be longer
But so far it's amounted to beans.

Few people will admit when they joined
A fad that's become of bitcoin
For they found when it's done
the value will plunge
Which feels like a kick to the groin.

Hunters:

When they go on safari
Let's hope they feel sorry.

The bullet train in California won't run
After costs became way overdone
It amounted to billions
Which peeved the civilians
So the finger pointing has now just begun.

Now it's a train to nowhere.

Many of the voters became mortified
With the ballots on assisted suicide
Yet fast as an eagle
They made it all legal
So let's hope the patients are satisfied.

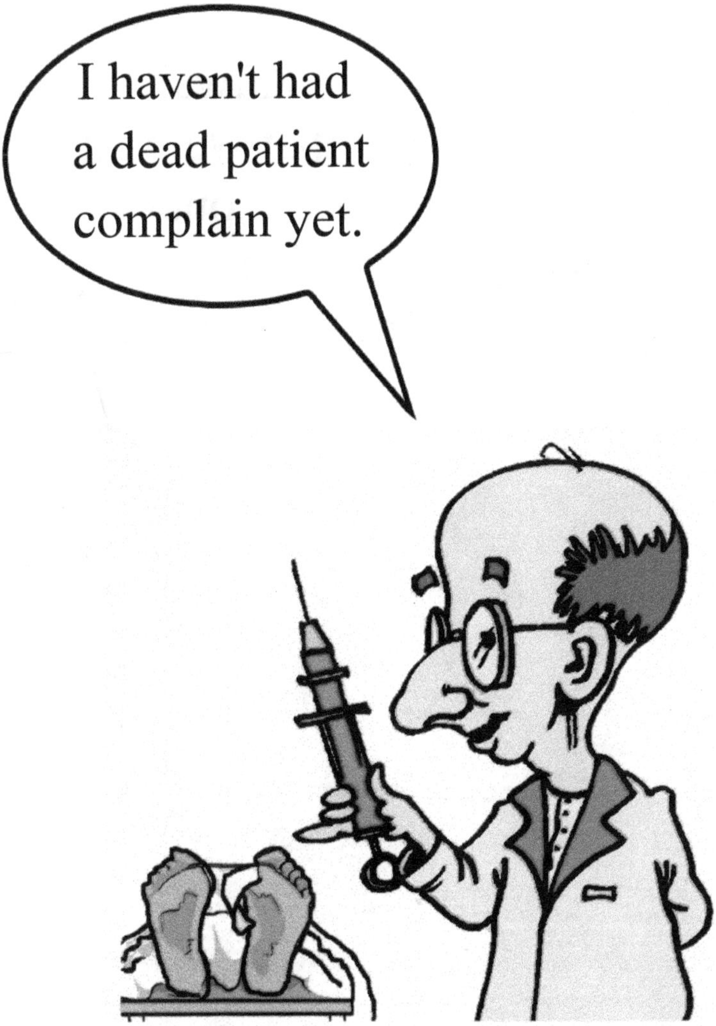
I haven't had a dead patient complain yet.

Why after the war in Kuwait
Did the army demand that we wait
When Hussein was the one
Still left having fun
Instead of boxing him up in a crate.

HEADLINE NEWS

Trapped boys in Thailand cave were rescued after staying inside for 17 days...

Question:

Should I really have my name on this book
Or am I more of a hamburger cook?

Security:

Why do they call them a safe
When they really should be called unsafe.

As our government was finally shut down
The Democrats were left with a frown
But after three days
The other side caves
And now they all look like a clown.

Guantanamo Bay was never closed
While the prisoners there still got hosed
Did our government fail
By leaving them jailed?
And what happens now, nobody knows.

When some children got trapped in a cave
A billionaire tried saving the day
So he build them a submarine
Which resembled a jelly bean
But instead they swam the whole way.

I wondered why no one's a critic
When talking about old Chappaquiddick
    Since someone there lied
    And someone there cried
While the cops were so slow and arthritic.

Word puzzles:

Washington once made up a mantra
On something they called Iran-Contra.

Caution:

When you hear about all of those studies
They're written by some of their buddies.

HEADLINE NEWS

A new study says eating pork makes you lose weight...

With so many protests on abortion
 It places my brain under torsion
  Yet each one who jives
   Came out alive
 If only that's kept in proportion.

"Did this topic really have to come up?"

They called it the Bridge to Nowhere
And it turned into quite an affair
Until funding was stopped
After the idea had flopped
So now we all need to beware.

Who knows what else is in here?

GPS has been helpful when driving
So people aren't late when arriving
But once it has showed
It picks a wrong road
Let's hope we end up surviving.

Question:

Why must TV commercials get worse
Until we ride in the back of a hearse?

Let us all rest in peace.

What's up with the bull run in Spain
It's like nobody's using their brain
If they go with the hoard
But avoid being gored
Some others will still feel the pain.

Class Action lawsuits:

The lawyers always act like the scholars
Yet always get all of the dollars.

Who has been to Tijuana
Where people do whatever they wanna
They drink and they smoke
With a strange language spoke
While outside it's hot as a sauna.

An ice age was once meant to come
Years ago according to some
But they changed their tune
After nothing came soon
So climate change is now what they hum.

Question:

Did the ozone once have a real hole
Or was it the size of a tadpole?

They once became a reality star
And thought that they'd go far
But after the show ends
They lose all their friends
So now they're out tending bar.

Statement:

I wish I had more to share
But my pockets are finally bare.

Finis.

www.ingramcontent.com/pod-product-compliance
Lightning Source LLC
Chambersburg PA
CBHW021955090426
42811CB00001B/43